Dear Bittersweet,

Anne Lai

Presentation by *BookLeaf Publishing*

Web: www.bookleafpub.com

E-mail: info@bookleafpub.com

ISBN: 9789357444965

First edition 2023

Hello!

I know you.
Ballerina brunette with an elegant gait
and lingering gaze, glinting gold richer
than your pretty polkadots of laughter.

Hints of crow's feet adorn dark honey eyes
that smile so wide, so kind–almost as kind
as the voice that brightens my blue.
I Know you.

Cloud Trails

You're from springs that web rugged forests,
earthy chaos
ripped from your roots by plane to chase a
dream.

I'm from painted pavements under monoliths,
brake light urbanite
hurried from home to chase that same dream.

And we talk about the dream that brought us
both here.

How you wear it like the dress your mother put
on a tomboy you:
dirty elbows poking awkwardly out of frills.

How I wear it like the hair tie of a ballerina's
bun:
temples taut, paying the price for prestige.

And the small spaces we find in the relentless
dream
to breathe, to break, to loathe, to ache,
to make oaths for our growth and not our
integrity forsake,

over silly things too, like
bubbles in jars and almond cupcakes.

Soft Summer Sunday

We took the road less traveled
with sprinkles of kisses from nettle,
sweating through collared shirts
and smelling trees of Persian Silk.

Spray cans of sunscreen,
tiny fingers in belly buttons,
choppy car rides with him asleep,
and French funk under tender discussion.

Then I spend hours on my floor,
spine and shoulders sink and snuggle,
dreaming to aimlessly explore
and taste the contours of the concrete jungle.

Can I Walk You to Your Stop?

Every time we speak,
I don't remember words–
just feelings.

Watch my worries wilt
in the shy split second
our eyes meet,

and a permanent smile
paralyze my sore cheeks.

Dark Mud

Your existence is a siren's shimmer in an
obsidian sea,
elegantly weaving into an ebony expanse,
skittering across steep swells
like the Sun through speckled shade;

like fireflies whose fairy hums
scribble fervent lines in the gloam of Midnight's
forest
only to settle in dewy tussles of sod;

like the wise trees that wail a baritone cello
moan
brimming of maternal desire–an aged and
wistful craving
heaving open mossy fissures for each fall of
Earth's breaths.

Untitled 32

When our eyes trade whispers
my bird heart flutters.
To be held in your collar's crevice
is for all she hungers.

Tread Lightly

I whispered that I hope our paths
cross again but I want
more than that I want
our paths to intertwine
to entangle
to embrace indefinitely

Parallel Realities

The time has come where our "x" becomes "="
–an asymptotic high-five, said someone at
twenty-one.

The arms of our paths won't even brush
no matter how much I rearrange the equation.

When the toll of church bells invades my ears,
you roll your eyes at traffic's trumpets on the
way home.

When vegetable roast tempts my nose away
from my desk,
coffee's electric linger follows you into work.

When a bitter one-dollar beer berates my tongue,
you wonder on a Wednesday what's left in your
fridge.

When my window's river rushes by to shush the
past,
your eyes whip to track the endless stream of
steel caskets.

And when I pull gentle gray sheets up to my
cheeks,
you rest fast asleep, twin mattress french kissing
the wall.

Our lines under the same sky; they might tango
and twirl but
never so much as touch. Why, what a tortuous
game I'd play
just to get close.

At the Bus Stop

Have you forgotten me already?

Soft shuffles of our steps to a shack made of
glass,
where our feet face each other,
where the tethers of our Together
entice Time to temper his flow,
though bus after bus will pass.

And when the sun ripens into the moon
I'll beg him to let me keep a sliver of the sky,

since the stars slither like sand through my
fingers.
Like a child who traces waves with a white
dandelion
only to find the seeds all sowed,
I believed the twinkle you tendered was mine for
keeping
but realized I wasn't owed anything.

Have you forgotten me already?

Shh!

They asked me what I saw in you
and I didn't know where to start,
your presence a dragonheart devout.

You asked what I write about
and I couldn't say,
wouldn't say,
didn't know how
to say.

Ah!

I'm losing composure
because I'm one step closer
to telling you how I feel.
It's itchy all over.

The absolute dread
of damning words unsaid
dare wrench my heart,
pick it apart I'm
so sorry.

I'll stay here for
as long as you need.
Godspeed and when you succeed
I'll be here on the floor,
flustered by my own turbulent war.

T-Minus 24

Such dissonance plagues each orchestrated
thought:
convoluted, depraved choreographies
of emotions forgotten.

All these compositions
–your compositions:
impositions on my disposition.

I'm afraid and ashamed
and allowed to hope(?)
So it is in my cathartic escapes
where I find rationed grief.

I already know the answer:
whale-sized swallow of tears to be.
To be what was,
what we were,
were we all I thought was worth
my million unspoken words,
my million thoughts not given
permission to breathe,
to see the world the way I see you?

I already know the answer.

Ouch.

You were the stake
driven into an itch,
stitched in place for seasons.
My skin started to seal,
to heal a home for the novel

until you ripped it out of its cavity.
My cells still search for the searing blade–
my flesh fruitless, hollow
awaiting the sickening red weep
that follows.

Watcher Above

Earthy expanse of enveloped emotions
crumpled, crippled, shriveled, stifled
into sorry splinters of salt.

You were
a slow billion year revoir, a grand orbit
around a dying star, a revel
in softly shimmering souls, and the dare
that dwells beyond the blackhole.

I've always been the one looked at, never
the one who looks.
So a nod to the gods, for now I know how
wonderfully profoundly it hurts.

Drumming Fingers

I cradle an intimate friendship with uncertainty—
her icy fog freezes still my feet, my pen, my
song.

Should I welcome her stiff embrace
or estrange a wistful mistake?

You're my moonstruck mindfuck,
candescent crossed stars of bad luck.

Your words spin in my mind like a broken
record,
each second guess a boisterously dissonant
chord.

And I'd melt in my misery knowing full well
I dwell in your permanent periphery.

The warmth of your hug fuels the fever in my
clenched jaw,
strangling each seething breath I draw.

But when the sun sighs her salutations
at least you'll have left me the gift of patience.

Good Morning,

When I woke up today
the gap you left
felt smaller and
I panicked.

How grateful I am to feel your heartache.
How grateful I am to have you to miss.

Words I'd Never Say

Not thinking of you feels freeing.
Not waiting for you feels relieving:

like I can breathe again,
like my feet can touch the floor again.

It's the cautious giggle with friends,
the cloudiness blinked away,
the candor of tomorrow and
the clarity of today.

I murmur this mantra at the back of a roaring
bus
when raindrops drum on smudged windows,
when fluorescent beams toss strangers' secrets
on an invisible stage
and our song waltzes in my ears like
the bittersweet sigh of a kiss.

Nigella damascena,

also known as Love-in-a-Mist,
Devil-in-the-Bush,
your favorite flower offered as a gift.

It tells the story of an emperor on a crusade,
drowned by a water nymph.
Fuzzy green blades of her hair sprout on the
banks
where his burbles bursted into violet stars. His
ghost starts
to wonder how hip-deep water claimed his
collapse,
how a sprite–dare he say siren–shouldered his
resistant relax
into unforgiving Turkish mud, though her
mirage
cradles his shrugging breathless cadaver.

I roll its stem back and forth between fingers,
the Sprite's hairs tickling, teasing my wrists.

I press it into a book so that the story lingers but
its purple petals were never mine to be missed.

Pedaling

I went on a date today and cried when I biked
home.

I wondered if I'd be redeemed if my mascara
didn't run
or so long as my twiggy tires still spun.

I wondered if the bird in my chest fluttered like
before,
or if I was the writer who claps her hands raw
for an encore.

They had the same dark honey stroking their
eyes,
the same dancing laugh, and effervescent
surprise.

And I wondered if it was a crime to look at them
like that
since looking away felt just as ill-willed.

But I also smiled on the bike ride back,
my heart beating a bit faster too, just not from
the hill.

Prints in Memory

I find your fingerprints everywhere:
on the pastel lichens that splatter tree trunks,
on the second song of my private playlist,
on the tongue of someone who tells me about
antimatter,
on the coy pouches under eyes that tell the world
of last night.

I find your fingerprints everywhere and I'm used
to seeing them but
I'm not growing around them.
They grow with me.
They stretch, spiral, wiggle, and warp
until they become the delicate torques of quilted
grain
that grace the oaky canvas of my being.

Your Sun in My Eyes

With her last breath
the Sun huffs her glowing embers
into the gods' softly brushed clouds
blanketing the dying sky.

She passes the torch to a lamppost.

He casts a mellow cone
into the purple mist of Evening
and salutes at ritual attention
for his giver's rubescent return.

www.ingramcontent.com/pod-product-compliance
Lightning Source LLC
LaVergne TN
LVHW050305200726

843509LV00015B/3177